The Tao and The Engram

A Tao Life Book

The Tao and The Engram

Structured Memories in a Brain
Volume I

Charles C. Lee

Writers Club Press
San Jose   New York   Lincoln   Shanghai

The Tao and The Engram
Structured Memories in a Brain

All Rights Reserved © 2002 by Charles Chulsoo Lee

Writers Club Press
an imprint of iUniverse, Inc.

For information address:
iUniverse, Inc.
5220 S. 16th St., Suite 200
Lincoln, NE 68512
www.iuniverse.com

This book does not guarantee enlightenment.

ISBN: 0-595-22465-2

Printed in the United States of America

This book is dedicated to Mom, Dad, Grace, friends, teachers, and random other organisms in the Milky Way.

The Tao cannot be left for an instant.
If it could be left, it would not be the Tao.

-K'ung-Fu-Tzu

CONTENTS

PREFACE

The Tao and The Engram represents the final product of a continually evolving process. In the initial phase, this book was designed as a treatise on Taoist philosophy. Then, it became enamored by the current state of affairs in neuroscience. However, eventually emerging was a collection of disparate work that seeks to answer a more fundamental question.

What is it about the memories in a brain that make us uniquely individuals? This is a question that has no definitive answer yet. Indeed, the dualists in the audience may argue that we are more than the collection of our experiences and our memories. Nevertheless, in perusing the accumulated experiences of other individuals we begin to see the parallel workings of other neural-state machines. Thus, with enough such exposure, we gain an intuitive understanding of the working of all such machines.

Are we more than the sum of our fractured memories? With that question, I leave you to enjoy the accumulated products of my neural-state machine. Let it add insight, or at least humor, into the function of your own neural-state device.

Charles Lee

ACKNOWLEDGEMENTS

I thank all of the individuals who have contributed to my current neural state.

LIST OF CONTRIBUTORS

Contributions were inadvertently provided by all those who have contributed to my current neural state.

CHRONOLOGY

About 27 billion years ago–The Universe was created

About 27 years ago–I was born

About a couple of months ago–I started writing this book

About right now–You're reading this sentence

About tomorrow–It will be ditch day.

Introduction

Are we more than the collection of our memories? Does our behavior reflect more than reaction to accumulated experience? Or, can our actions be treated as the simple functioning of a neural-state device? Questions such as these continue to puzzle philosophers and scientists. And although the answers continue to elude inquiry, alternative approaches are available.

The Tao and The Engram brings together a collection of work designed to answer a philosophical question. The engram is a theoretical construct describing the biological storage site for memories. It is currently believed that different types of memories are stored in vastly different locations in the brain. So, what if we were able to separate emotional memory from logical memory? Motor memory from cognitive memory? Will the individual be more than the sum of the parts?

In fact, there is no way we can really tell the answer to these questions. And, I don't really intend to provide one. However, as an exercise for myself, I have assembled several items that I have written over the years into one volume. I have grouped these into different categories based on an intuitive feel for how they were produced. In theory, this should be a hard copy of my neural state, or in other words, my engram on paper.

However, this should not be read as a treatise on the engram, or taoism for that matter. This is simply a compilation of work that I have written over the years. Some of it is good. Some of it is probably not so good. But, if you read it all, then you should have some insight into my neural state. Then again, maybe you won't. Really, that's up to your neural state.

I've divided this collection into pieces based on anatomical structures responsible for the storage of separate memories.

The Amygdala is a structure that is believed to be responsible in the short-term storage and consolidation of emotional memories. In particular, it is involved in fear-based learning. I've stretched the definition to include several works of prose that I wrote. These were written free form, and are perhaps the closest things I've written to pure emotion.

The Cerebellum is a structure that is involved in the coordination of motor activity. The collection of musical pieces for guitar could perhaps be included in the section on the amygdala, but music is an inherently more active process. Chord definitions are given in standard tablature notation.

The Left Cortex has been described as the logical brain. As a result, I have included several essays that I have written in science in this section. What could be more logical than science?

The Corpus Callosum is a bundle of fibers interconnecting the two halves of the cerebral cortex. I have included transition pieces on science humor in this section.

The Right Cortex has been described as the emotional brain. Here I have included some works of humor that I have written over the years. What could evoke more positive emotions than humor?

Currently, it has been suggested that the brain acts as a neural state device, with activity from all of the structures in the brain contributing to a given state at a given time. Thus, it is unlikely that separating out the separate works into this formalism is necessarily informative. But, if your neural state can reintegrate this information in a unique way and winds up being inspired to greater things, then my neural state will be overjoyed for yours.

Enjoy.

The Amygdala: Prose

ALAS

Alas, those halcion days of bygone summers churn against an effervescent cauldron of burning desire and lost youth. Feel how swiftly life prevails upon our yearning for a glimpse of the eternal while groping always for the succulent and ephemeral.

Our lost dreams.

Our lost hopes.

Our lost feelings teeter against the precipice of our eventual demise, and struggle against those who forge a forsaken destiny. We, who have sold our souls for a moment's bliss, realize all too late of our imprisonment in the fleeting progress of chaos.

LAST RIDE

Onward and upward, railing through a ladder of infinite possibilities with nothing more than the shadow of death hanging bluntly overhead, the great dearth of humanity diverges into a split stream of consciousness like an eternal slumber driving the futile churning of an effervescent cauldron. These men, these refugees, from that last sorrow which has forsaken them, through what aperture do they view their existential meandering on that pointed road to the reaches of infinity, effortlessly struggling against a dimensionless reverberation of those nociceptive feelings that bleakly counters their innocent stares? To what end does it concern them? Let them follow in that darkness and let their sorrows fade into an emptiness that resides in all but those lucky few who have actualized their dreams. Oh, those fortunate few who have prevented their potential from slipping away like unmitigated fodder throwing forth its flora and fauna as it kicks and screams into a trenchant struggle that each is predestined to lose. So, continue onward! Consider it as though the purpose of some greater good were to be had. Surely, even those hypocrites among the throng must realize that especially in the eternal dark abyss, only a tumultuous upbringing of redemption can possibly await.

But, look around you lads! What redemption resides in the vast, bleak scope of eternal ebony's last ride through the wilderness? All around they must see the transformation of that righteous reality into a perilous state which has no knowledge of the road to oblivion. Yet, only on that road can they find their hopes, their dreams, and their sorrows as they slowly march in blissful ignorance on the trek to that land which offers only the faintest hope of salvation from themselves. But, do they not know that such salvation can only be granted by imposition of those taciturn beliefs

4

into a world misguided by their existence? Who are they? These men, women, and children consider less in that upbringing and resign themselves even less to enduring it. These few who choose to lash out at the oppression caused by those single-minded beliefs and erstwhile fantasies. These few who rebel against the dearth of understanding caused by those fools. Cry out, oh Absalom, and realize that life has not one shred of understanding, but only a glimmer of release. Discover, oh caustic beauty, and embrace the once proud eternity surrounding us as the last seed withers away. Plead, oh winsome youth, and struggle one last battle for eternity's end. Only then, in all these lies, will your praise be uplifted.

BOWER

Once more, sanguine resolution preordains the plight of our fancy. Last cries of the infinite yearn at the promise of corned beef and cabbage. Gathering its momentum towards emerald Nick. Outweighing briefly the last dance of forever. In celebration, perhaps. More likely, the drunken stupor of portentous folly.

Bleakness. Dissonance. Surrounded in this world of hopeless remonstrations by the blinding sutures of eternal moribund ineptness. To save us, only the promise of celebration. Yet, our intertwined fates conspire once more, and this erstwhile existence led once again astray. To what excuse can I owe our misfortune? Only to the yogurt of our demise

UTAH

Direct your attention heavenward and see that god that we have created struggling for a glimpse of infinity. That sallow, jaundiced yearning caught in a moment stretched outward as it toys with the dying embers of a thousand, sullen supernovas, creating forever a moment frozen for eternity's earnest ending, and revealing the recollected awakening to a dappled morning dew. Recall, one morn, those barren, sullen fields of Utah's sinuous countenance as it stealthily crept inward into the glory of an ill-prepared sun. Cautiously, the wistful warmth tightened it's grasp, and in that moment, time expanded outward with the unparalleled force of countless lives branching from the nodes of an aeolian ether. The fury of nature's fusillade evinced that the time of reckoning within the soul had become a landscape replete with the culmination of so many lives bought and paid. Oh, those hues of amber and rosemary which coveted this barren vista! Barren no longer by electric realization winding its grasp into the fiber of being. Life held precariously eternal in a moment so suddenly slipping away. That moment when all was right becoming ever less recognizable. So suddenly gone as though never in my grasp. Just a faint glimmer. A memory. As if it never existed. Much as I don't now.

MEANDERINGS

The ethereal beauty of the morning sky spread out before me on the wings of gossamer beams. Unlike the previous afternoons, the days had been filled with an unknown wanting for a life that I could not find. Unknowing, I stood before the great pane glass window, its silvery sheen glistening and reflecting that ghost of an image that held my countenance. Outside, a great oak meandered its way towards the heavens in search of knowledge. Knowledge of course unlike that which we could comprehend, for the knowledge that a tree seeks is perhaps only of value to those external gyros that power this great cosmic cinder that we call our home. But, the recalcitrant nature of the oak in its waning beauty this early fall shadowed a measure that was wholly left to be unseen. Whether it took pride in its austere beauty in the glimmer of the sun, or whether it thought of the ages past when it was but a mere sapling has eluded even those whose powers to perceive such matters transcend the boundaries of this corporeal existence in its entirety. Whether even in its sapling state, it had any inkling of the cosmic forces dancing about that brought order from disorder and stature from chaos will remain forever a mystery.

But, so I stood pondering the issue itself. I did not question the mood, but rather accepted it as the whim of some unseen force driving me towards a greater end. Naturally, of course, I realized that this could not be true. All about me was the evidence that showed otherwise. The thresher's flail and the like. But still I stood peering at the oak and wondered to what magnificent state it had arisen. What events had transpired around its massive frame that had changed the course of a tiny insignificant fraction of this cinder's local inhabitants. Nature knows no boundaries in the questioning of such ideals. All powers in one and all in unity. The notion that what we are is but what we perceive ourselves to be.

I slumped on the bed despondent, its soft cavernous embrace enfolding my aching head. It did of course do little to sooth the deeper spiritual ache that enraged the passions of all fair maidens whom I had passed that previous day. For on first sight, a maiden is a lovely creature, flawless and infinitely pure.

Everyone an angel.

Everyone sent from god.

The disparity between the ideal set forth by god himself and the reality that that same god had in fact engendered and brought into physical reality surprises me to this day. Yet, how utterly boring we would find it to discover that our ideals had been met. That our pallid, shallow sense of perfection had been met. That which our obstinate minds perceive as perfect. Great beauty was though to exist in the perfect drawing of a circle. But, oh how it pales in comparison to the multivariate structure of that aging leaf as it trickles through the air on its last flight towards earth. To of course assign the roll of god as being the arbiter who created all things to his sense of perfection is once again an argument that even the soft embrace of this downy soft pillow can not abate.

BLAZER

In bitter moments of unrepentant despair, the last dawn weeps slowly over the remnants of those earthen shadows whose pallid vision casts an ominous glare over the glory that once was, but is now no more.

Weep not for his innocence.

Sing no requiem for his grace.

Shed no tears for his grandeur.

Let the world only hear the tortured presence of such memories torn asunder in an instant, scattered through the crystal spectacles of a life's ill-spent meandering.

RAPTURE

Ah sweet rapture! What blessed thoughts have found their way into a mind unprepared for an assault so sanguine? What penetrations into the nocturnal dimensions of one so blissfully unaware? That here amongst the throng of unbelievers there was one. If only in that time the swiftness across the ages revealed their preternatuaral scheming, the rapidity with which our feelings slide across an ocean of doubt might forever be quelled. So then do the haunting of our earnest queries eternally embrace that fleeting look and that innocent stare. The realm of possibilities unfold like a thousand supernovas burning within a space filled bleakly by our inter-mingled glares. It was the eyes. Like a thousand angels dancing in the pallid shadows of an aged Venus. It was the breasts. Like two limpid duccets cast absently in a trodden field. It was the hair. Broadcasting their delicate glissendo across eternal ages. What feelings are shared in an erstwhile laugh with only sorrow welling in those eyes betraying enchantment? What happiness is found on that long trenchant struggle filled with doubts without comforting embrace? It is merely the carelessness of that demeanor fueling the dying embers of a life not meant to be. Think not of eternal laughter. But only of the sorrow in whose arms our destinies await. Think not of glorious summer. But only of the somber scope of a blissful winter morn. Rejoice not in childish glee. There is only that demise which we shall never overcome.

ONCE MORE ALONG THE RIVER

Undeterred, I stood out in the evening glare of the waning moon, its perfunctory glance shining down on me with that characteristic, perspicacious demeanor, as if of some great aegis whose purpose has eluded every probing of those insane and hungry enough to try. Standing, I felt those long strands of nightshade, whose whispers danced playfully in the lilting breeze. Before me, the river stretched into the distance, toying with the recalcitrance of the shear rocks that maintained their steadfast legion, but whose numbers slowly diminished against the overwhelming onslaught of the river.

In the distance, I heard the passing of the freight train as it trundled on its long journey carrying the daily burden of men's toils. The sweat still glistening from their heavy, laden bodies as they plunged headlong into the river to cleanse not only the brief carapace that housed their vitality, but perhaps also something more substantial housed deep within the inner recesses of that convergence in space and time where angels fear to tread. Dare we say that even in this brief moment when the river washed away what was left of their innocence, perhaps it gave them back the lost distractions that so often men forget they have had.

Yet, still onward into the depths of the waning moon, the freight train protracted the consummation of its tireless journey, not really considering what it had left behind nor the methods to which it had left its own marks on the daily burdens of society. It carried its own sense of being and purpose with it. Onwardly moving like the ebb and flow of the river that writhed alongside, journeying towards that slipstream which would inevitably ride it out to the great expanse that awaited. Such single-minded persistence winding down that omnipresent pacemaker that times the futile cycle of their intertwined existence. Doomed to repeat their daily trudge for as long as those chaotic equations that govern us all continue to plod out their positions along the great expanse.

But what of it?

The river in whose bosom the men wash away their toils holds little regard for the tumultuous past and the turbulent future. And the engine plodding along with its daily load should scarce sacrifice a moment on such pithy considerations. Yet, the never ending basking in the river as the engine moves overhead continues unappeased.

PRECISION

Precision in a glass so iridescent.
The realm of possibilities.
The world freed of life's lot reconsidered.
The tepid demeanor of her cold glaring stare.
The dissonance crowding modalities.
Her smell like a Beethoven symphony.
Her look like a chocolate whispering embrace.
Her perfume like the blue on an evening rain.
The swirl of throbbing mindless stares.
The yearning.

TRIBULATIONS

Spellbound, I quickly regained my composure as I prepared to address the enchantress who had so suddenly urged her way forward. "Oddly, the evening's shade suits your demeanor", said I with a pretense of disinterest and a dollop of nonchalance. Yet, her steadfast glare pierced heavily into my bosom's soul as those streams of light slithered down from the heavens and bestowed upon her that ethereal glow that truly tries men's souls.

Enraptured by such beauty, I professed unto her, "But, what of the nature of our mutual existence that slips and slides it's way through the years, searching for that promise of a perfection that perhaps we might never find, only to see it now hanging on our every word, just out of reach, an instant apart, yet a millennia away."

Quickly, I recoiled with horror into my own mind at the absurdity of the suggestion, and searched desperately for those words that might lead back unto salvation. Yet, the pebble had so emphatically been hurled into the river. Even now, those ever expanding waves rippled out to fan the flames of desire. Truly, this wandering vixen with her daily wares must have it right, her considerations lasting but an instant, and her attention now turning adroitly to more attractive game.

I sighed heavily. Perhaps it is not the nature of this life to wonder about such matters. Perhaps it is only the loss that we feel. Perhaps the yearning for something greater than ourselves. Is it? Or is it the life which we once thought we were to lead but whose emphasis has now shifted so dramatically? Such eternal questions can only find themselves trapped in a vicious cycle eluding our earnest queries. If only we knew the loss which was beholden to ourselves, and if only we were confident in that true instant in which we reside, perhaps those inner demons which possess us might break loose and reveal themselves to be no more than those shadows of the past rapidly encroaching upon our daily lives. What of those demons? Do they feel the pain and suffering which they have thrust on to this futile existence? Do they pride themselves on the job well done? Do they announce that yes indeed they are the lords and masters of the domain which we personally no longer have free range over?

Perhaps.

Perhaps.

Perhaps.

But, could it be that in that moment's instant in time, a moment forgotten to all but those steadfastly unaware, we might slip sideways into that abyss which surrounds us all and on which we are all precipitously perched. Patiently awaiting the lies to fill that chasm which stretches infinitely beneath us, so that we may once again walk tremble footed on those tenuous tendrils that support our facade. But, oh how easily they shatter and tumble down. And, oh how bearable it would be if the inevitable torrent of inequity only shattered the hopes and dreams of the ones who built them. Yet, the corruption of all those who took stock in those lies proceeds unabated as well. For such is the nature of the abyss to destroy the lot of ourselves in eternal procreation

DISCONSOLATE

Dark held dappled beneath effervescent light. Ahead of me an iridescent rainbow of sound. The manner proclaims this fact of life, only seeing rare beauty so suddenly standing.

Our existence standing alone, yearning for fate forgiveness of sins. Realizing those fates earnestly sought destroy the vast expanse of the possible.

In a million realities, which venture is down?

No one but ourselves.

Long ago, we gave up such pernicious entreaties as the preternatural clockmaker forced the erstwhile chosen. Forgive them of their sins. They should not know this road. They rely only on the mapmaker's omnipresent journey.

One with no end.

The horizon glimmering succulently with rasp gustatation eludes the yearning bosom. We plead for its sanctimonious denial of ourselves, but never appease that whim.

Leave it be.

The essence of our lives.

NEVER AGAIN

Nocturations revealed perfunctorily.
Temptations cross the corners of infinity's last ride,
Bowing to machination,
Turmoil,
And seething effluvia?
Awaiting the true.
Joy.
Pain.
Mostly pain.
Sometimes joy.
Joy so fleeting.
A life so sanguine not found.
Searching for lost trivia.
And the unworthy found.
Listen to the birds of summer.
As they dance in deep blue air.
Sing with me.
Feel the eternity?
The epoch of life held in zest.
Do you see it?
Do you hear it?
Does it reverberate the soul?
Yearning for expression.
Feel that.
Struggling.
Never again.
Never again.

BRINY

So what of your eternal gratitude? So what of that meaningless flight into the bliss of apotheosis? A bliss easily torn asunder by the fecundity of an ignorant few. Their insanity castigates our lost struggle. And that art of procreation, that residue of god, yearns for life at fulcrum's end. But Oh Destruction! That tumultuous uprising of a tortured soul churns against this river's edge, peering across fractious temptations amidst brackish waters of finite resolution. Assassinations lost among the turbid salinity of this briny raconteur. Do you see that lost child? Lost in life's tsunami. Crying at our gains. Weeping for our fortune. Dying at our success. Unleashed once more for feats against even stalwart hearts!

The Cerebellum: Music

WALK AWAY

CHORD DEFINITIONS:
Am   002210
C   030210
D   200232
Em   022000

INTRO LICK
```
B———-1—3—1—0————————
G—2———————————-0—2—
```
Repeat while strumming Am

INTRO
Am   C   D   C   (x3)

BASS RUN 1 on Last C of PROLOGUE
```
A———3—-2—-0—
```
to Am with Intro Lick

VERSE 1

Am	C	D	C
Here's my	part of the	grand old	story
About the	fight for	love and	glory
About a	man and	his true	love
Broken	hearts in	high	above
Aya	Baya	Soo Na	Na
Aya	Baya	Soo Na	Na

23

BASS RUN 1

INTRO LICK

VERSE 2

Am	C	D	C
Every	time I	see her	face
It's calling	me to the	same old	place
Dashing my	hopes out	in the	sky
Begging for	the answers	to reasons	why
Aya	Baya	Soo Na	Na
Aya	Baya	Soo Na	Na

BASS RUN 1

INTRO LICK

CHORUS

Am		Em	
And I don't wanna		know	
And I don't wanna		show	
And I don't wanna		hear	
And you don't have to		fear	

Am	Em	Am	Em
'Cause I'm	not gonna	let you	walk away
No I'm	not gonna	let you	walk away
No	Oh	not	away
No	Oh	not	away

GUITAR SOLO 1
Pentatonic in Am over Am-Em change in Chorus
End with
BASS RUN 1 followed by INTRO LICK

VERSE 3

Am	C	D	C
It could have	been one	big ro-	mance
Stars above	and a	big slow	dance
But my poor	soul was	far too	yellow
And so it	never	said	hello
Aya	Baya	Soo Na	Na
Aya	Baya	Soo Na	Na

BASS RUN 1

INTRO LICK

CHORUS

GUITAR SOLO 2

CHORUS 2

Am	Em
And I don't wanna	know
And I don't wanna	show
And I don't wanna	hear
And you don't have to	fear

Am	Em	Am	Em
But now	you've gone	and walked	away
Oh now	you've gone	and walked	away
No	Oh	not	away
No	Oh	not	away

INTRO LICK (x2)

OUTRO

Am	C	D	C	Am	C	D	D	D	Am

INTRO LICK (No chords)
end on Am

UNLIKELY: AN ESCAPE INTO PARADISE

CHORD DEFINITIONS

E5dim6	032400
Bdim3/G	320400
E5sus4	002400
E5sus4(add2)	004400
Bm	224432
F#m	244222
Fm	133111
G	320033
A	002220
Asus2	002200

INTRO:
E5dim6   Bdim3/G   E5sus4   E5sus4(add2)   (x2)

VERSE 1:
E5dim6   Bdim3/G
Here I am now baby   you tell me to be true.
E5sus4   E5sus4(add2)
I don't love you no more and you don't love me too
E5dim6   Bdim3/G
It's like that fried up piece of stuff you left upon the ground
E5sus4   E5sus4(add2)
A whole lot worse than all that crud and all your lousy sound

CHORUS:

Bm		F#m	Em	G	A	Asus2	A Asus2
It's un-	like-	ly	you're gonna know				
It's un-	like-	ly	you're gonna show				
It's un-	like-	ly	you're gonna grow				
But it's so	like-	ly	I'm gonna go and get a real life				

E5dim6   Bdim3/G   E5sus4   E5sus4(add2)   (x2)

VERSE 2:

E5dim6   Bdim3/G
Like a rollin' thunder ball you filled me with your thoughts
E5sus4   E5sus4(add2)
But, I no longer give a hoot 'cause lies are all you brought
E5dim6   Bdim3/G
And if you think the two of you can hurt me with a look
E5sus4   E5sus4(add2)
Then you don't know me baby so watch out for the hook

CHORUS(x1)

MIDDLE 8

Bm	F#m
And I don't	know
And I don't	care
And I don't	want you
if I have to	share

(repeat once)

CHORUS (x2)

OUTRO:
Same as intro.

A Midsummer's Run Around

CHORD DEFINTIONS

C	032013
Gsus4	320013
Fsus2	x03213
Am7	002010
Am7(add6)	002013

INTRO LICK

```
E——————————3—
B——1—3—1——————— (x2)
```

INTRO
INTRO LICK over C

VERSE 1

C	Gsus4	Fsus2	Am7(6)
I'm running around	town to	trying to find my	way
from	town,		
Trying to see where	I belong and	what I'm meant to	be
Is it for me to	ask myself	or is there just no	hope
I'm searching for	And life just	away	
answers I can't find	passes		

BASS RUN
A —-3—2—0—

FILL 1
Am-Asus2-Am Fmaj7-Fmaj7(sus6)-Fmaj7 (x2)

CHORUS (pick up on Am)

C/B	C		C/B	Am	Asus2
					Am
And	Now I'm		living the	never	
			life that I	did	
And	My is it		never the		it was
			same as		then
And	Where is the place I'm gonna		be at home		
'Cause	All I've been looking for I can		never find		
Yes	All I've been looking for I can		never find		
No	All I've been looking for I can		never find		

GUITAR SOLO 1
Use FILL 1
into 2/3 I up to 2/3 III then 2/3 V
for F G Am
Am pentatonic solo with 2/3 V then progression down
Am G F into INTRO

VERSE 2

C	Gsus4	Fsus2	Am7(6)
I've stopped in places	I once knew	and had a look	around
Things were the same	but I had changed	and so had my	point of view
I'm still not sure	where I belong	or what I'm meant	to be
I guess I'll never	figure it out and	that's what's	killing me

BASS RUN

FILL 1

CHORUS

GUITAR SOLO2
(as Guitar Solo 1)

CHORUS

OUTRO
Same as Intro and end with Intro Riff(no chords) followed by C chord open E in treble.

TOMORROW

Capo 1

INTRO
Am G

VERSE 1
Am G   Am
Oh   Tomorrow…Can I ever see the rain before   tomorrow?
Em   Am
Cause I alone for us I kept our   sorrow
Em   Am
And I alone I sought the road less   traveled
F   Bb F E Am
Can I find a way?

33

VERSE 2
Am   G
Oh   Tomorrow…Can you ever see the rain before   Am
                                                                  tomorrow?
Em   Am
Cause you alone for us you kept our   sorrow
Em   Am
And you alone you sought the road less traveled
F   Bb F E Am
Can you find a way?

INTERLUDE
Am   Fmaj7 (x3)
F(bar)   G(bar)

CHORUS
C   G
Baby don't   you ever cry
Bb   F
Time's a lark   lets ask not why
C   G
In the end   we'll feel the same
Bb   F
Cause in the   end no ones to blame
C   G
It won't ever cross our mind
Bb   F   Am
Living life   I know we'll find
Fmaj7   Am
Tomorrow

INTERLUDE

VERSE 3
Am   G   Am
Oh   Tomorrow…Here will see the rain beyond   tomorrow
Em   Am
Cause we alone we'll keeps our only   sorrows
Em   Am
And we alone we'll find the road less   traveled
F   Bb F E Am
Here we'll find a way

INTERLUDE

CHORUS

OUTRO
Bass run on
A—-3-2-0—-
ending on Am

HESPERUS

CHORD DEFINITIONS

Bm	224432
F#m	244222
G	355433
A	577655
B	799877
F#	244322
D	557775
C	335553

INTRO

B   A   G   F#   Bm

Pause and tap guitar for four beats

VERSE 1

Bm   F#m

Long before the   Hesperus wreck

G   A

And long before   I knew

Bm   F#m

Long before the   days of old

G   A

When you and I   were cool

Bm   F#m

Long before we   both had met

```
G                        A
and I was still      a fool
Bm                         F#m
Long before we      both had met
G                        A
And I had dreamt         of you
```

BRIDGE
```
B                    A              G              F#
It was not the       days of old    that kept me in  my shoes
And it was not how  we first met    that made me    feel alone
And it was not you  standing there that kept me in  my shoes
'Cause if you want  to feel my pulse its beating    without you dear
```

CHORUS
```
D                        A
Now I'm              feeling great
C                        G
Baby I got           to run
D                        A
Everything           is feeling fine
C                        G
And the sun          is on behind
D                        A
Now I'm              feeling great
C                        G
Baby I got           to run
D                        A
Everything           was feeling fine
C                        G
but your back upon my mind
```

FILL
A   G   F#   Bm

VERSE 2
Same as verse 1

BRIDGE

CHORUS

OUTRO
Same as FILL

The Left Cortex: Science Essays

GROK AND THE VANGUARD OF SCIENCE

Set against the tumultuous backdrop of the 1960's, the publication of a single novel hardly seems notable. Yet, the debut in 1961 of Robert Heinlein's novel, <u>Stranger in a Strange Land</u>, remains a landmark in the history of science fiction. In one sense, it foreshadowed the emergence of a counterculture whose dominant repercussions still resound in the popular mindset. But perhaps more interestingly, it introduced into the lexicon the term "grok".

Definition: grok (gräk) *v.* To perceive a subject so deeply that one no longer knows it, but rather understands it on a fundamental level.

The novel spins the tale of a Martian visitor acquiring knowledge about the earth, its history, and its cultures. However, despite accumulating a wealth of information, he still is unable to "grok" the earth. Similarly, science is in the business of acquiring knowledge about nature, its rules, and its principles. Unfortunately, like the man from mars, science still is unable to "grok" some fundamental issues regarding the nature of the universe.

Take for instance quantum mechanics, or the laws of physics at very fine distances. Although physics can transcribe the rules that quantum particles obey, it is unfortunately reticent on the actual meaning of these rules. Or, look at the recent sequence of the human genome. In a large sense, it represents a mere catalogue of information with little understanding of its biological implications. Finally, take one of the biggest mysteries, human consciousness. Although a wealth of knowledge about information processing in the brain exists, there still is little to be said on how the brain gives rise to conscious experience.

Despite the multitude of scientific achievements in the past century, knowledge still remains confused with understanding. Although the practical results of scientific endeavors may not require such a deep understanding, it is at least important for furthering an intellectual appreciation of our place in the universe. Hopefully, with the vanguard of science on the march, these deeper scientific issues will soon be grokked.

NEURAL-MACHINE INTERFACES

Vision, audition, somatosensation, olfaction, and gustatory sensation. The construction of our world view strictly depends on these five sensory modalities. A deficit in even one of these abilities leaves a deep abyss in our appreciation of the finer points of life's sometimes ambiguous meanderings. Imagine the loss of the sight of an iridescent sunset, the smell of a redolent rose, or the sound of a brilliant opera. For many, this undesired reality has become a fact. And for all, the gradual declines in perceptual abilities emerge as the years begin to finally chip away on bodies that no longer recover so easily from the assault of time. To alleviate these deleterious conditions, the creation of artificial devices for sensory perception has become a tantalizing prospect. And attempts to create such devices must rest on both a secure knowledge of the input required for the system and the processing of this information by the brain.

In my perspective, there are several key research areas that will play a role in the development of the technology required to create these sensory devices, including biomaterials science, electrical and mechanical engineering, neuroscience, and bio-organic chemistry. In particular, neuroscience and bioengineering will be crucial.

Neuroscience seeks to explain behavior in terms of the underlying physical mechanisms in the biology of the animal, and then reintegrate that information in a theory of behavior. These questions regarding mechanism will reveal methods for intervention when problems arise in the system. In principle, it is here that the bioengineer and bio-organic chemist could play a key role in creating synthetic neural devices to replace the defective biological systems. As appropriate biosynthetic methodologies emerge, molecular and cellular tools could create biological systems that could interact with appropriately designed artificial sensory devices. While speculative, I believe that it is a reasonable goal. The solution requires a two-fold approach. First, there must be a detailed understanding of the neural mechanisms underlying sensory information processing in the organism at many levels, i.e. the systems, cellular and molecular levels. Second, this mechanistic approach must incorporate a consideration of appropriate biosynthetic analogues that can replace defective sensory systems at either the systems or molecular levels. Only then will a 'true' artificial sensing device precisely mimic the ability of the innate biological system.

THE GENETIC CODE: HISTORICAL CONSIDERATIONS

The history of science is replete with examples of paradigm shifts that have led to new ways of dealing with old problems. In considering the progress of scientific thought, it is often instructive to examine these paradigm shifts, not only for their historical value but also as models for future shifts in thinking. In such a study, we hope to be able to gain insight into how such change in the scientific community occurs. To this effect, there are several well-studied examples, such as the case of Galileo and his evidence against a geocentric universe. Contemporary history also provides us with several examples of changes in scientific thought. Notably, we find several of these instances occurring in the history of molecular biology. The fact that this field of study is relatively young has several advantages. Most notably is the fact that there is a good historical record and first hand accounts may often still be available. Consequently, studying the major events in the development of molecular biology should be invaluable in the consideration of the paradigmatic shifts. To this end, we consider one of the major breakthroughs of the century occurring in molecular biology, the breaking of the genetic code.

The history of the breaking of the genetic code derives its existence from work performed by many sources. We begin our consideration with the development of the genetic coding concept. The coding concept owes its existence to the refinements in the genetic concepts of a basic unit of heredity, the gene, which specifies the genotype and the phenotype which is a physical manifestation of the genotype. Over time it was realized that the gene was expressed very simply through the production of a protein species which was characteristic of the one gene. Thus, the one-gene-one-enzyme hypothesis was created. Further refinements of this concept was attained when it was realized that the gene itself is composed of DNA and the protein is composed of amino-acids. Furthermore it was eventually realized that the DNA and proteins were composed of linear sequences of nucleotides and amino acids, respectively. It was believed and eventually demonstrated that there was co-linearity among the sequences of the gene and the protein. Thus, the genetic coding question was eventually formulated. In effect, how does the gene map its information from its DNA sequence to the sequence of the protein.

With the question detailed, a rush of ideas proposed ways in which the genetic code transferred its information. As can be seen from the early ideas, many of the hypotheses regarded the breaking of the genetic code in mostly cryptographic terms, or as a logic puzzle. This was understandable owing to the innate feeling that nature should operate in logically and clearly codified ways. Indeed, it should in many respects. However, as will be seen, early consideration of the genetic code almost completely ignored or misinterpreted certain basic physical requirements of the coding apparatus. Consequently, they were doomed from the outset.

One of the earliest notions to have wide spread effects on scientific thought regarding the genetic code was a hypothesis set forth by George Gamow. Gamow was himself not a biologist but rather a physicist. He brought a physicist's outlook to the problem and concluded that one could determine the genetic code based on numerical relationships and without much experimentation. Although such approaches to the problem were common in theoretical physics, it was ill suited to the task of deciphering the genetic code.

Gamow's first hypothesis was his diamond code hypothesis. He based this hypothesis on the Watson-Crick model of the DNA strand. He noticed that certain diamond-shaped pockets could be found in this model. These pockets were formed from a base on one-chain, the adjacent base pair, and the next adjacent base on the opposite chain. Gamow proposed that amino acids would directly bind to the pockets formed by the diamonds and in some manner be connected together to form the protein. In his model of diamonds coding for an amino acid, there are 64 possible diamonds that can code for an amino acid. However, the number of classes of diamonds is in fact 20 owing to degeneracy because of order independence. Since the number 20 is generated from this model, it appeared that each of the twenty different amino acids could associate with one of the classes of diamond structures. In addition, the spacing between diamonds was found to be very close to the spacing between amino acids in a protein, 3.4A to 3.6A respectively. Due to the numerology and apparent structural evidence, this model was very attractive.

However, problems naturally existed with this coding concept. First and foremost was the fact that this code was fully overlapping. In effect, the starting base of one diamond was immediately adjacent to the starting base of the next diamond. However, a fully overlapping code puts obvious mathematical limitations on the number of possible sequences that can be constructed. It was thus shown from calculations and experimental evidence that sequences existed that were not compatible with Gamow's code.

Despite the problems of the diamond code, it nevertheless established several important precedents that we find in later coding concepts. One of course is the notion of an overlapping code that we have previously discussed. Second is the notion of a single basic unit in the DNA for coding, eventually called the codon. In addition, he established the concept of a uniform codon size for all the amino acids. The idea that degeneracy, or more than one codon could code for a certain amino acids, was inherent in the model. We also note the previously hypothesized co-linearity among sequences. Finally, there is a generality in Gamow's coding concept which extends his code among all living things.

Still, the diamond shaped code was not Gamow's only attempt at cracking the genetic code. After the failure of his initial attempt and an increasing awareness of RNA combined wuth the fact that it should have some role in genetic coding, he revised his theory to what was called the triangle code. Like the diamond code, the triangle code had a codon size of 3 base pairs and it retained the notion prevalent at the time that the amino acid must interact directly in some manner with the template. However, it differed in that the code itself consisted of a tri-nucleotide segment not a diamond that coded for the amino acid. Once again, he was able to produce degeneracy that reduced the 64 combinations to 20 classes coding for the amino acids. And he allowed the code to be partially overlapping such that it was possible to incorporate more sequences. This hypothesis had mixed support from various experiments and was never fully dismissed until much later with the Nirenberg-Matthaei experiment.

Another of the important early contributors to the idea of the genetic code was Francis Crick. He proposed a model that was on the whole different from the one set forth by Gamow. Crick noticed that it seemed chemically improbable for amino acids to combine directly with the DNA. There seemed no way in which the multivariate side groups could be distinguished or even bind with the DNA directly. Consequently, he proposed an adaptor hypothesis which in essence stated that there must be some intermediate which binds both to the DNA as a template and the amino acid. In hindsight, this was a remarkable prediction to make at the time, and it also had far reaching consequences. Since if the amino acids do not associate directly with the DNA but rather with an adaptor, it seems suggested that the association of an amino acid to a specific codon is not a predetermined event in the evolution of the genetic code. Regardless of this facet, the adaptor hypothesis gained acceptance with the characterization of the tRNA molecule that had all of the essential characteristics of the proposed adaptor.

One of the off shoots of the adaptor hypothesis was that it created a situation where if an adaptor is sitting on the template then another adaptor has no choice but to bind adjacently in a non-overlapping manner. Thus, the code must not be overlapping. Yet, a fundamental problem to the nature of a non-overlapping code is that multiple reading frames exist, i.e.

three for a codon size of three base pairs. This feature of the adaptor hypothesis was troubling, since one should wonder how the cell is able to choose the correct reading frame to use. To this end, Crick proposed what is now called the comma-free code as an explanation. If one could construct a code which consisted only of codons such that no codon could exist as an overlap codon, then the problem would be solved since only one reading frame is possible in such a situation. For example, if the codon ACA is in the code, the codons containing CA* or AA* (where * is any base) are not permissible since such codons could also be found in overlapping codons. For a triplet code, it turns out that a coding size of 20 codons is generated which contains no overlap codons. Thus, 20 codons were generated which could code for 20 different amino acids.

The 20 codons appearing in the generation of the comma-free code helped to bolster the comma-free code. Indeed, because of its appealing numerology, the comma-free code quickly supplanted Gamow's hypotheses and soon became dogma to scientists studying the field. For nearly five years, the comma-free code influenced much of the thinking in the coding field until the experiment of Nirenberg and Matthaei disputed it. Once again, the problems with the comma-free code was that it still regarded the problem of solving the genetic code as merely a cryptographic one. Consequently, it made incorrect predictions by attempting to force a code onto nature.

As was stated before both Crick's and Gamow's hypotheses were dismissed by the work of Nirenberg and Matthaei._When compared to the other approaches being developed for trying to break the genetic code, their work proved to be a relatively simple experiment. It determined a simple codon assignment using an in vitro system containing all the amino acids and a poly-U strand of DNA along with the requisite chemical machinery. The result of the experiment was the production of a polypeptide strand of poly-phenylalanine.

The fact that the UUU codon was undoubtedly coding for the phenylalanine completely dismissed the idea of a comma-free code since a UUU codon is itself fully overlapping. In addition, the experiment completely finished off any lingering doubts regarding Gamow's direct template hypotheses. In addition, this and further experiments where other bases were incorporates served to help establish the coding size, co-linearity, and eventually the degeneracy of the coding apparatus. Eventually, the entire code was worked out through further experimentation and the presence of start and stop codons helped to elucidate the reading-frame problem faced by Crick. Yet, the initial experiment by Nirenberg and Matthaei demonstrated the importance of solving the code by treating the situation as a physical one that must be probed to derive at an answer.

What we observe from the gradual shifts in thinking from Gamow to Crick and then to Nirenberg and Matthaei is a slow change in the approach to solving the genetic code from dealing with symbols to one dealing with a biochemical problem. Indeed, we must admit that both Gamow and Crick recognized certain physical aspects of the problem. Yet, they still eventually reduced the problem to the cryptographic one treating the bases and amino acids as mere symbols on paper. The realization of how to tackle the problem as more than mere cryptography was a slow one owing in part to the mathematical and logical appeal of the coding schemes developed in this way. And, in the end, they finagled a way of producing a variety of contrived coding schemes and imposed them on nature rather than allowing nature to dictate the rules.

THE OLFACTORY CODE: CURRENT CONSIDERATIONS

A rose by any other name still smells as sweet.

—Shakespeare

Among our myriad of sensory inputs, olfaction is perhaps one of the least appreciated, not only in terms of the subjective value of its relevance in daily tasks, but also in terms of the objective, scientific understanding of the mechanism by which olfactory information is encoded and processed. This dearth of understanding extends across neural, cellular, and molecular levels, and is undoubtedly due to the common perception of olfaction as something of an expendable trait. Nevertheless, the utilitarian values of olfaction should not be marginalized. Regulation of a number of important physiological functions depends on the proper functioning of olfactory receptors and neurons, not the least of which is appetite. In addition, the strong emotive and associative abilities of odors have been well characterized in both the scientific literature and in prose like that above.

As a biochemical problem, the neural basis of odor may be even more intriguing. Even though it is possible to predict with some regularity the physical properties of small molecule compounds that are synthesized in the lab, it is still impossible to predict whether or not a synthesized compound should smell, and if so what it should smell like. This is confounded by the fact that a chemical analysis of odorant molecules fails to reveal any obvious rules. It is indeed common to find compounds with similar structures that smell quite different, and compounds with vastly different structures that smell the same. Unique receptor-odorant interactions may account for part of this ambiguity.

The problem is several-fold. In order to understand the larger phenomenon of "smell", an understanding of the coding and processing of information in the olfactory system is required. However, breaking the fundamental "olfactory code" appears to be far more difficult than in the other sensory modalities. Ideally, one would like to begin at the systems level where a general principle organizing the encoding of sensory information in the peripheral areas for vision, audition, and somatosensation is an arrangement of receptors essential to that modality in a topographically defined manner. For instance, the retina contains neurons topographically arranged such that their response properties are determined in part by a correlation with an object's location in external space. However, such a topographical delineation of parameters in the olfactory periphery and cortex has eluded researchers.

Interestingly, much of the peripheral circuitry suggests that such a map may indeed be present. Olfactory sensory neurons presumably expressing one type of receptor converge onto specific glomeruli, where interactions with neighboring channels are sharpened via lateral-inhibitory circuitry. Consequently, a putative center-surround receptive organization may exist in the mitral output neurons. But, if so, what defines the center and the surround? Indeed, the difficulty in defining the parameters in such a map are readily apparent, and arises from an incomplete understanding of the chemical determinants, or "odotopes", which are processed at the molecular level of the olfactory receptors. Put into biochemical parlance, the biophysical interactions that underlie the binding of the odor ligands to its cognate receptor are unknown.

Therefore, essential to unraveling the "olfactory code" is an understanding of the ligand-receptor interactions at the olfactory receptors. Dissection of the molecular determinants at each receptor that gives rise to its specificity for cognate odor ligands should yield insight regarding the chemical information transduced by the periphery and transmitted for processing by the brain.

Until relatively recently, attempts to break the "olfactory code" at the molecular level were stalled because the receptors involved in the transduction of chemical odor information in mammals were completely unknown. However, the cloning of a family of putative odor receptors in the rat by Buck and Axel revealed an unknown class of seven-transmembrane, G-protein coupled receptors (7TM GPCRs). In humans, it was revealed that some 500 to 1000 different genes comprising an estimated 1% of the genetic information are spread throughout the genome. The identification of the receptors allowed for a molecular dissection in the rat of the patterns of expression of the receptors. And, although there appears to be topography of the projections from the rat olfactory epithelium to the olfactory glomeruli, the actual distribution of receptors in the epithelium is random.

The affinity of the odor receptors for ligand has been hinted at with recordings from neurons which show broad profiles of responses to different odors suggesting that each neuron either expresses one receptor with broad specificity, or expresses several with narrow specificity. This has only recently been elucidated by functional studies of overexpression of odor receptors in the rat epithelium. Until this point, none of the putative odor receptors had been definitively linked with a cognate ligand. In the case of the OR-I7 receptor, affinity for n-octanol was determined including broader specificity for a range of structurally dissimilar compounds. In the chemoreceptive homologue ODR-10 in *C. elegans*, high affinity and specificity for 2,3-butadione, pyruvate, and citrate were shown while excluding structurally similar ligands varying in hydrocarbon length or functional units. And in the OR-5 receptor expressed in the baculovirus/Sf-9 system that reports on G-protein activity using a biochemical second messenger system, specificity for aromatic aldehydes implied selectivity of binding but not specificity.

In short, olfactory receptors appear to have a unique property in that individual receptors have broad specificity for structurally diverse ligands. This broad specificity at the level of the receptor is of particular interest since it may underlie some aspects of the "olfactory code" which determines the nature of a smell. In addition, this property also appears to separate the olfactory receptors from the pheromone receptors, which are believed to have highly specific interactions with a single pheromone molecule. As an aside, pheromone receptors appear to belong to a different superfamily of proteins and are sequestered in neurons that are part of a different sensory circuit. Regardless, understanding the biophysical and biochemical interactions of the olfactory receptors with its ligand is essential to unraveling the "olfactory code". However, determining the nature of the actual interactions requires more direct biochemical approaches than those employed by previous researchers.

Devising a method for rapidly screening the known olfactory receptors for cognate ligands readily calls upon a molecular genetic approach. Previous attempts to link putative ligands with this approach have relied on the heterologous expression of a few known receptors in tests for binding. One such study using HEK 293 as the host cells revealed three previously unknown ligand-receptor pairs. Yet, these approaches suffer from the limited scale of their search space. To take a purely combinatorial approach to the problem, one would like to test all of the known receptors simultaneously for binding affinity to each odorant.

In this regard, a number of systems have been described that are suitable for the heterologous expression of olfactory 7TM GPCRs. Perhaps most interestingly is a system that makes use of the yeast pheromone response pathway. By coupling the heterologous receptor to the pathway, the downstream components can be utilized to signal the binding of a ligand to the receptor. Typically, the assayable response is the growth of cells on restrictive media. However, the reporter gene could in principle be replaced with one that produces a readily visualizable signal, e.g. betagalactosidase or GFP.

Thus, the rapid combinatorial linking of olfactory ligands to cognate receptors can be accomplished through this procedure. However, these low-resolution pairings need to be verified through alternative means.

The limitations imposed on structural studies of integral membrane proteins are notorious. Much of the difficulty arises from the characteristic hydrophobic regions that cause increased difficulty in purification, solubility, crystallization, etc. Indeed, the only structure of the family of 7TM GPCRs known to reasonably high resolution is that of bacteriorhodopsin. However, biochemical studies on related 7TM GPCRs, such as the beta-adrenergic receptor, have revealed corroborative evidence of similar structures in related family members. Due to their large number and diversity, the olfactory 7TM GPCRs offer a unique opportunity to examine the variability in the protein scafold underlying these types of ligand-receptor interactions. Therefore, revealing these underlying interactions is not only important to the issue of neural coding, but also to the larger issues of protein folding and evolutionary genetics.

Interestingly, an empirical understanding of the biochemical interactions underlying the interaction of odor receptor and ligand has only recently been accessible with the development of suitable bacterial expression systems for functionally expressing soluble, purified protein in large quantities suitable for analysis by biophysical methods. The development of a system utilizing the baculovirus/Sf9 expression system to drive expression of protein allows one to obtain a yield of 20 mg of protein from one liter of culture. Preparation of receptor is relatively straightforward. Specific mutations are made that stabilize the seven helix bundle without affecting the ligand binding domains, and a purification tag is added, i.e. His-tag, FLAG-tag, or GST-tag. Protein is produced and sequestered in the inclusion bodies of the bacteria, but is readily solubilized with detergent and purified by affinity chromatography. The protein is then reconstituted into liposomes which recovers the binding activity. This system can then be used to construct and produce a number of native and mutant receptors to study the relevant contributions of various residues to the binding energetics.

In a study of the OR-5 receptor using molecular modeling with bacteriorhodopsin as the template and lyral as the bound ligand, structural residues putatively involved in establishing the receptor's specificity for ligand were identified. In this receptor and presumably all members of the family, the transmembrane helices are oriented around each other in a counterclockwise fashion as viewed from the extracellular side. Six loop regions are present that alternate between the intracellular and extracellular space and which connect the seven helices. These helices form a central pore that creates a binding pocket that brings together the key residues necessary for the binding of the ligand and subsequent transduction of the signal.

Helices III-VII each contribute residues for binding with Tyr 278 on Helix VII implicated as being the most important energetically for binding to lyral. Presumably, this is due to a hydrogen-bonding interaction between the hydroxyl group of the tyrosine and the carbonyl group on the lyral. More interesting are Phe 206 and other residues on Helix V whose sequence diversity across cloned receptors implies a mechanism for tuning the range of odor sensitivity.

As seductive as this model is in providing a structural basis for odor selectivity, independent verification of the model is essential, since a structure calculated for one receptor and one ligand on a bootstrapped template undermines the true diversity necessary for the range of receptor specificities. Other theoretical studies have furthered corroborated the importance of the residues on helices III-VI. In one, the use of correlated mutation analysis, a method whereby several of the receptor sequences were analyzed for residues that mutated in tandem, implicated residue. In particular, His 430 and His 426 are of particular interest because the imidazole side chain can act as either a hydrogen bond donor or acceptor. It can also form electrostatic interactions as well as forming hydrophobic contacts. This versatility in the number of interactions could account for the broad specificity.

Further refinement of the initial models has been carried out using amino acid variability profiles of the growing number of sequences across species. These have refined the position of the binding site to a cleft centered between helices III, IV, and V, and further implicate helices IV and V as important in providing a structural basis for odorant binding. Although, the implication in comparing with the previous experiments suggests that these helices may be important in a general selectivity for odorant, where residues on the other helices are involved in fine-tuning of the selectivity, as in the case of Tyr 278 of the OR-5 receptor. In addition, a refinement of the residues putatively involved in the overall stability of the receptor revealed important stabilizing interactions, such as putative disulfide linkages and helix stabilizing residues. Although not important to the issue of receptor specificity, it is useful to the larger issue of the stability of transmembrane proteins in general.

Therefore, the construction of an expresed using site directed mutagenesis of a number of key residues. In particular, His 430 and His 426 are of particular interest because the imidazole side chain can act as either a hydrogen bond donor or acceptor. It can also form electrostatic interactions as well as forming hydrophobic contacts. This versatility in the number of interactions could account for the broad specificity of the odor receptors.

If indeed the olfactory periphery is acting as a feature extractor of chemical information, what features are being extracted? Several factors suggest precision in the computations occurring at the level of the olfactory glomeruli. The convergence of projections from sensory neurons expressing a particular receptor onto one glomerulus and the presence of apparent lateral-inhibitory circuitry indicates that information is indeed sharpened before transmission to higher stages of processing. This suggests that perhaps a spatiotopic map exists at this stage and contains an unknown representation of chemical space.

In considering the structure of olfactory receptor-ligand interactions, the applicability to the broader question of olfactory information processing must be kept in mind. Supposing that the structural determinants of the ligand-receptor interactions are revealed empirically, what does this imply for the larger hedonic sensation associated with smelling the odorant? Indeed, the aforementioned broad specificity of these receptors suggests that the combined activity of several receptors each with different affinities for an odorant may contribute to the overall sensation. In which case, an investigation of the biophysics of the interactions these other receptors may also be required.

These considerations have broad implications in a number of fields. Neurally, these ligand-receptor interactions will define the range of substrates that the system will deal with in its computations. Biochemically, these different structures will yield insight into the structural constraints on proteins which mediate ligand-receptor interactions. And genetically, this data will yield insight into how evolutionary pressure builds a repertoire of receptors from duplication of receptors in the olfactory epithelium.

In short, although the chemical sense of olfaction may be the most primitive in evolutionary terms, it may be the most complicated in terms of understanding the biochemistry, molecular biology, and neural basis of the sense. Indeed, one only has to compare the number of receptors subserving each modality to see the complexity evinced at even the molecular scale. Perhaps through the specific dissection of one particular odor across several levels of analysis, the "olfactory code" will finally begin to be revealed.

The Corpus Callosum: Science Humor

GENETIC CLOTHING OF HUMANS

Supported by a Grant from the National Institute of Hats (NIH)
by a Donation from the Clothing Institute of Technology (CloTech)
and by viewers like you.

Recent events in the world of genetic engineering have brought to light once again the real possibility of cloning humans. Naturally, this has sparked a great deal of discussion and debate; most of which has resulted in the successful formation of several committees with unpronounceable acronyms.[1] However, should the cloning of humans become a reality, we will be confronted with the even greater dilemma of finding suitable attire for the cloned humans to wear, what has been termed the "genetic clothing problem". The significance of this problem was recognized in earlier work by Ward et. al. when it was deduced that "clothes make the man."[2] Consequently, cloned humans can not be considered true clones without suitable accompanying dress wear.

In this regard, there have been significant advances over the last century by researchers in creating cloned apparel for the everyday human. Indeed, the progress in this field has been so successful that garment diversity has steadily decreased over the past century as the industry has begun to breed single stock lines.[3] Still, the process has proven to be inherently imperfect, and even among specific lines of clothing, small imperfections leave the unforeseen possibility that each article in the line might retain some degree of individuality. Therefore, we suggest that this cloning process be further refined such that these trace amounts of individuality can be effectively eliminated.

In addition, various ethical questions have been raised regarding the cloning of human attire. These arguments are evinced by the "eugarment" experiments that produced plaid shorts and bell-bottom pants. To this, we counter that judicious, reasoned use of the process that is approved by at least fifty governing bodies and Hanes Inspector #12 could effectively circumvent a repeat of such activity. We are confident that the timely implementation of this plan will allow the cloned humans to enjoy the same healthy level of mediocrity which we pride ourselves on today.

Next, we shall consider the efficient cloning of the television sitcom…

---

[1]   See National Bioscience Advisory Committee, and the Council forResponsible Genetics.

[2]   Ward, M., A. Sears, P. Roebuck, J.C. Penny. 1997. The Summer Spectacular Blowout Sale. *Sunday Circular.* 12:1-4

[3]   See Nike, Levis, and Guess. 1980. Shirts, Jeans, and Shoes: Identification of the Putative Requirements for Service in a Restaurant. *Office Max Business Supplies Catalogue.* 42: 21-2

HEMOGLOBIN

In the beginning, God created the heavens, and the earth, and a whole lot of blood. But, he wasn't quite sure what color it should be. He thought, "My my. Red is a lovely color. It reminds me of blood," which was actually something of a paradox, since he had yet to give blood a color. But, who am I to argue with the mental processes of the Almighty? In any case, God then looked around and began to admire his ass that was a mighty beautific shade of blue, owing to the fact that he is God and his ass is perfect.

Now, God wishing to create man's ass and blood in his own image was in something of a conundrum…which is odd since this brings to mind the question of "Is there a question that even god can not answer?" Anyway, this was not one of them, since he instantly hit upon a solution.

And so on the sixty-ninth day, God spoke, "Let there be blood that is comprised of hemoglobin whose heme moiety can bind oxygen to take to the cells so that it can be used for aerobic respiration. And let the hemoglobin be a brilliant shade of red when oxygen is bound, such that the cells will forever know that they are about to receive the Eucharist for which they must forever thank me?"

And it was so.

Then God spoke once more saying, "Does anyone have a cough drop? All of this ordaining is giving me a sore throat."

But lo, there was no Circle K open on the sixty-ninth day.

Then God spoke once more, "Fuck this shit. My throat is dry and my ass is blue. What kind of jacked-up, bullshit operation are we running here? God damn it. Oh that's me. Well, this will not do at all. So, just to jack things up even more, let the hemoglobin turn into a brilliant shade of blue once it has delivered the oxygen to the cells and replaced it with carbon dioxide. Thus, the arteries that carry the life giving oxygenated blood shall be red in eternal praise of my loveliness, and the deoxygenated blood in the veins shall be blue in eternal praise of my sore throat and blue ass."

And it was so.

Then god said, "Well, that's taken care of. Now get me two, red-hot mamas and three tickets to a Vegas show staring Urkel!"

But lo, Hooters was not open on the sixty-ninth day.

...

And when the church elders read this first draft of the Bible submitted by Henry the Prevaricator which included the above bit, they said, "You know Henry, the bit with the guy dying on the cross was pretty good. And that part where he gets up again was pure genius, everyone is still waiting to hear what you have planned for the sequel. But, this bit about the Hemoglobin has just got to go."

Well, when Henry heard this, he was incensed. He immediately got up, turned around, farted, and left the room. Despite this setback, Henry kept persevering. And today, we all know him by name, since he is the founder of the largest chain of restaurants selling refried beans, thus proving that your ass may be brown, but your blood will always be blue and red.

QED

The Right Cortex: Humor

The Quicker Picker Upper

Well, Folks, Ol' Uncle Chuck has arrived to help you out of the doldrums with what promises to be an interesting series of vignettes on the weather phenomenon known as El Nino. But, let me tell you right off the bat that I'm not going to be one of those lecherous uncles whom everybody hates and whom everybody tolerates just because he's got wicked huge barrels of cash. Not that anyone really keeps their money in barrels…well, maybe except for Mormons and those retarded guys who live down the street. Interestingly, 4 out of 5 dentists can not tell the difference between the two, yet they prefer the retarded guys hands down for getting their teeth sparkling clean.

This of course brings us back to my first point. Well, actually it doesn't. But, who's going to stop me from saying so? You, punk? I thought not. Anyway, God himself has chosen me to be the next Spice Girl…the Funkadelic-Curmudgeon Spice…and he has also asked me to write to explain life, the universe, and everything. Frankly, I thought the subject was just a little bit too dull. I always thought that we should be covering more interesting topics, you know, like selling crack. Interestingly enough, the proper selling of crack is an art form that has fallen by the wayside ever since the Spice Girls released their first album. It is of course my personal belief that historians will look back on that act as being the impetus that sparked the decline of Western civilization. This of course led to the rise of a new civilization of highly intelligent piles of dung…genetically engineered by the ingenious cross-fertilization of a dung heap, two retarded guys, and a dentist. It was an act that was universally condemned at first, because like all truly monumental discoveries, genius is never appreciated in its time. Eventually, it was awarded the Nobel Prize in Dung Science.

But, of course, by that time the piles of dung comprised 80% of the voting members of the prize committee. Oddly though, in this new civilization, human rednecks continued to thrive, mostly because they were the only one's who were winning the Publisher's Clearing House Sweepstakes. And of course, the Spice Girls continued to ride the top of the charts, because the rednecks and the piles of dung were the only ones who were listening to that crap in the first place.

Seriously though, it's not that I don't like the Spice Girls. It's just that I think they suck. Not, that sucking is necessarily a bad thing. It can be a good thing if done in the proper manner and in discrete locations on the body, preferably those near body orifices. And, it's not that their music is terrible. It's just that it sucks. Besides, whenever I listen to a track off of the Spiceworld album, my hair spontaneously combusts. Never mind the fact that the CD player is next to a Bunsen burner aimed at my scalp. There's no correlation. Hey, if you want to hear good music, go out and buy one of Hanson's albumns. Mmm Bop. Mmm Mmm Mmm Bop. Yeah Yeah Yeaaaaah.

Well, as you can tell by now, Will Shakespeare…this article ain't. A raving mad man who uses Mormons to get his teeth sparkling clean…this article be. But as we have all learned from our study of television sitcoms, the first few episodes always tank big time as the writer fumbles to develop the characters into something more than two-dimensional stereotypes. But, we also know that the one thing that will save any episode is the Stupid Guy/Neighbor/Barman/etc. making a dramatic entrance…

{STUPID GUY ENTERS IN A ZANY FASHION THEN PRAT FALLS OVER THE COUCH. HE SPRINGS STRAIGHT UP AND LOOKS STRAIGHT INTO THE CAMERA. (That's a real no no in television, but who gives a fuck. This is my show.)}

STUPID GUY: Hoo Ha Ha. Hello Folks, I'm The Stupid Guy. Expect to see me in future episodes doing all sorts of zany stuff. Hoo Ha Ha. And, of course, bursting into brilliant one-line sound bites that you'll be saying to all your unhip friends who don't read this article, like Hoo Ha Ha. And, of course pushing the running gag until it's as dead as Baby Spice's Hair-do. Hoo Ha Ha. Have fun kids, but remember…wash your hands after going to the bathroom and don't eat dung. Or else you'll wind up like me…The Stupid Guy. Hoo Ha Ha.

{STUPID GUY EXITS IN A ZANY FASHION BANGING HIS HEAD ON THE DOOR ON THE WAY OUT. LAUGH TRACK KICKS IN ON OVERDRIVE.}

Well kids, Uncle Chuck has got to go. El Nino is continuing it's rampage across the United States treating America like a cheap two dollar hooker that's having a going out of business sale. Remember, buy two blows and get an extra special helping of crack absolutely free! Farewell and remember…Don't Eat Dung.

{This Message brought to you by the Presidential Sub-committee on Hookers and Dung Eating…a lobby of PepsiCo and RJR-Nabisco}

$160

Last night began like most nights, with the stench of the homeless permeating the air. Deciding to venture out into the decaying streets of Berkeley, I was stopped by one of the city's fine, citizens driving a car that would have spoken if it could.

"Hey buddy!" he shouts from his dilapidated auto, "Want to buy a laptop?"

Intrigued, I shout back, "How much?"

Quickly, the car pulls over and after the customary inquiries regarding my possible employment by various law-enforcement agencies, he opens the back of his trunk to reveal several boxes of laptops.

"Pentium III! 500 MHz! CD/DVD Player!" he proclaims turning the box around and showing the list of features. "$300!"

"Hey, buddy. I can't afford that," I reply trying to haggle, "How about $100?"

"Ah, come on! Help me out here! " he says while nervously rubbing his lucky rabbit's foot, "Look at my wife…she's pregnant. How about $160? I can give you a deal for them all. I gotta get rid of them tonight, man!"

"Urr..Uhhh…Ummm…Okay. $160. I just need to try and get the money. Wait right here, and I'll be right back!"

Racing home, I awaken my roommate from his peaceful night of slumber. After explaining the situation to him, he admonishes me for being an idiot and advises against the deal, yet he still agrees to front the cash.

Returning to the scene, the deal goes down swiftly. Hyped up by the sheer exhilaration of illicit activity, we race home to open the box. But, as the wrapping is slowly pulled away, the true horror of the purchase becomes painfully evident. Embedded within the box is….

A BRICK!!!!!!!

Which reminds me of a little de-motivational poster...

MISTAKES: It may be that the only purpose of your life is to serve as a warning to others.

So, this concludes today's lesson/warning: "How to Become an Idiot by Giving Your Money Away."

Formerly titled: "Paying the Stupidity Tax: Every Citizen's Responsibility."

EAST TIMOR

EAST TIMORESE GREET GRACIOUS GENEROSITY

EAST TIMOR (UPI)–After weeks of bloodshed and genocidal mass executions, the East Timorans were thrown a welcome lifeline from the Golden Pacific Brewing Company. The company known for its prolific dealings in international politics, human rights, and fine beer manufacturing has announced yet another Monthly Free Beer Party! Immediately following the announcement, months of political, social, and sexual tension ended in a collective shrug.

Commenting on the recent spell of altruism, one company official stated, "East Timor? Dude, is that like some wicked awesome ale?"

International experts are still puzzling over what effect this announcement will have on relations between East Timorites, Indonesians, and millions of overweight, American beer drinkers.

Nevertheless, the East Timoritians were indeed jubilant following the announcement of yet another Free Beer Party. In the words of one of the blighted citizens, "I've lost a brother, both of my arms, and my ability to procreate, but I will raise my feet in praise to the pagan god that I worship and thank him for creating the Golden Pacific Brewing Company!"

The world will now look on anxiously as the East Timorinians recover from months of oppression, slaughter, and a raging hangover.

THE NATIONAL AGENDA

FREE BEER: THE NATIONAL AGENDA AND SOCIAL POLICY
FOR THE NEXT MILLENNIUM.

Free Beer. What does it mean to you? For some, it reflects the high moral values on which this country was founded. For others, it brings to mind a utopian world free of death, disease, and poverty. But for those degenerate few, it represents a naked conga-line led by a slightly tipsy, triple-breasted whore of Babylon.

For over a thousand years, the Golden Pacific Brewing Company has committed itself to improving the moral, social, and political landscape of the nation. The company has achieved national recognition for donating cases of its elegant Golden Stout to the impoverished youth of inner city schools. It has been highly lauded for providing bottles of its sublimely smooth Dark Ale to underprivileged, nursing mothers.

Most recently, it has received a glowing endorsement from Jesus of Nazareth whose organization has recently begun serving the delightful brew during the Eucharist as part of its efforts to "spice up" the blood of Christ.

In the words of the Almighty, "I've tasted a lot of beer in my time, but the Golden Gate Pale Ale is the best fuckin' shit ever, dude!"

ELIAN

ELIAN TO USA: "FUCK OFF!"

HAVANA, Cuba (AP)–Amidst a sea of turmoil and stupidity, Elian Gonzalez faced reporters today to issue a final statement.

"To all of the people in Miami and the United States," the statement began, "Fuck Off!"

What followed was a barrage of expletives lasting more than twelve hours, which left many political pundits scratching their heads, and many political pedophiles scratching their testicles. Experts, who up until this incident didn't have a job, have concluded that this outburst was in response to the Golden Pacific Brewery's recent price hike of $5 for their monthly "Free" Beer / "Free" Food party. The ramifications of this price hike were first felt last month, when inebriated, stock market investors were forced to sober-up and dump all of their useless internet stock.

In support of Elian's statement, crazed-dictator Fidel Castro proclaimed over state-controlled radio, "To all of my lowly citizens, you may live in fear that you will suddenly be abducted, tortured, and killed by the state police, but I promise that the beer in Cuba will always flow freely."

Following the announcement, beer prices rose sharply to $200 a bottle.

MONEY

ANNOUNCING AN AMAZING MONEY-MAKING OPPORTUNITY!!!!

FOLKS!!! What would you say to me if I told you that YOU could be earning anywhere from ONE to TWO whole dollars a month!!!

"CRAZY!" you say????

"INSANE!" you say???

"FART!" you say???

Billy Blank's "TAE-BO FOR PROFIT" can't guarantee this!!

"AB-FLEX YOUR WAY TO RICHES" can't guarantee this!!

Not even "RONCO'S ELECTRIC DEHYDRATE YOUR WAY OUT OF DEBT" can offer this kind of deal!!!

But, you may be asking yourself, "What can the Golden Pacific Brewing Company, which offers fine, fine beers at low, low prices at the end of every month, teach me about financial security???"

Well, Paco! That kind of independent thinking is the sort of free-spirited behavior we will teach you to destroy in OUR program!

So, Send NO Money!

Don't Act Now!

Supplies Are Plentiful!

And, I would have gotten away with it too if it hadn't been for you meddling kids!

EXISTENTIALISM

MODERN EXISTENTIALISM, BEER, AND SAUSAGES: A RE-EVALUATION BASED ON RECURRENT, NONSENSICAL, SEMANTIC PROPOSITIONS

Ontology. Epistemology. Eschatology. To some, these words underscore fundamental distinctions in the construction of a coherent worldview. To others, these words belie a greater truth defining the nature of self, free will, and theistic propositions. But to most, these words are associated with the pompous, self-important pricks with nothing better to do in their spare time than contemplate the futility of existence and the vacuousness of the cosmos.

In redefining modern existentialism for the new millennium, most modern beer drinkers have rallied around the new proclamation, "Cogito Ergo Sum....My Ass!!!" Leading this new school of thought is the Golden Pacific Brewing Company, which has been instrumental in introducing the terms "Pale Ale" and "Heffeweissen" into the current lexicon.

No longer is it possible to argue the relative merits of Dostoevsky's "Notes from the Underground" without first conceding that the Golden Lager's bitter aftertaste results from the brewery's fine choice of hops and yeast. Nor is it possible to dissect Nietzches' influence in antebellum Germany without a craving for Aidelle's Louisiana Spiced Sausage.

Embracing the current shift in thinking, most philosophers have echoed Kierkegaard's 1923 statement: "I may live in a godless, desolate, inhospitable universe where bad things happen to good people, but THANK GOD for the Golden Pacific Brewing Company!"

TIGER

TIGER DOES 'IT' AGAIN!

BOTSWANA, NJ (AP)–Former internet porn star and cult leader, Elderick "Tiger" Woods, has done 'it' again! Indeed, not since the likes of child actress Dana Plato have the millions of starving Croatians had such a force to rally behind.

Commenting on 'it' at a press conference tomorrow, Woods will be reported to have said, "I can't believe I did it! I didn't think I had it, but then it happened. It's the greatest thing to have happened since the last time it happened, which by comparison wasn't really as good as it was the time before that. Or, that time when...", and so on for another twelve hours.

Not all were as surprised as Woods by 'it'. Deceased Teamster and current head of the Golden Pacific Brewing Company, Jimmy "Let Him Ferment" Hoffa, has reportedly attributed 'it' to the brewery's monthly beer and sausage party, which also has recently been held accountable for rising gas prices, and the annual rotation of the earth about the sun.

"Glug, glug, glug," said Hoffa's disembodied head.

On the other side of the Mississippi, wary church officials, though not officially commenting, have carefully not ruled out exorcism.

"Although we are reasonably sure that the creamy, rich, and flavorful Golden Gate Pale Ale is responsible for it, we can not rule out a pact with the Dark Lord, or even worse, a competing brewery. Either of which would require a swift kick to the nads," said Pope John Paul II in a prayer to God.

BANGLADESH

BANGLADESH MAN DIAGNOSED WITH EGOTISM

COLLEGE STATION, TX (AP)—Once endemic only to prosperous nations, the deadly blight of egotism has marched across the globe faster than an internet dot-com declaring bankruptcy. Today, in the wetlands of the Bangladesh desert, the disease struck once more. The afflicted man, Watssa Matta Yu, 38, was described by doctors as being "a total, absolute, fuckin' prick."

Watssa, a slave-laborer for Nike, recently became afflicted with the disease after his promotion to Head Shoe-Sniffer. Since that time, he has reportedly displayed the classic symptoms of strutting, boasting, and vaunting.

The Bangladesh strain of the disease appears particularly virulent. Classic treatments of mocking, shunning, and belittling have proven hopelessly ineffective. Fortunately, the Red Cross has rushed to the scene with several cases of the Golden Pacific Brewing Company's Amber Ale and Golden Bear Lager.

The Brewing Company, long known for its humanitarian efforts against apartheid and its ability to deflect earthbound meteors, has generously donated its silky smooth beer to ease the suffering of Watssa's co-workers.

The people of Bangladesh quickly erupted with tears of joy following news of the donation. In the words of one of Watssa's beleaguered associates, "Sure I work 26 hours a day in dank, oppressive conditions, while that insufferable prat gets to sniff the shoes BEFORE they urinate in them, but thank god for the Golden Pacific Brewing Company!"

THE BIG FIGHT

IT AIN'T FAULKNER...

Ol' Joe sat by the river all day. He dreamed of the big fight. Often, we would go down to the river and say, "Hey Joe! The big fight is comin' soon. Ain't it?"

Joe would smile and say, "Soon. Very Soon."

Those were the lazy days of summer in Alameda county. Not much happened there as a rule. But, this year was different. This was the year the Package came to town.

I remember it well. The brown van trundled into town carrying the year's supply of hog swill, corn feed, and of course the Package. It pulled up to Jack's Place and the loosely uniformed driver stepped out with his clipboard in tow. He wiped the sweat from his brow, adjusted his cap, and strode through the dilapidated front door.

Jack looked up from the corner bar stool, put down his Snapple(tm), and nodded to the stranger. "I reckon' ya got the Package we all been waitin' fur."

"Yup. I reckon' so."

. . . .

Much of the day had soon passed and the sun was drifting toward the horizon. Ol' Joe wandered down Yonatapetwa street and heard the commotion emanating from Jack's Place. Deep within him, he knew this was the day. He sauntered into the bar and the crowd parted a clear path to the newly delivered, finely balanced, precision engineered, and grossly over-priced Keg of the Golden Pacific Brewing Company's Amber Ale.

Tears streamed from Ol' Joe's eyes and I heard him mumble, "Other than my wife, it's the most beautiful 4 feet 340 pounds I e'er laid my eyes on."

He shuffled up to the keg, pulled out his mug, and gripped the pump tightly. Then, in a move that startled all those around, he leisurely keeled over and died. Some say he died of happiness. Them fancy doctors say he died of cirrhosis of the liver.

Ol' Joe never fought the big fight, but the big fight lives on.

ZEAL

RELIGIOUS ZEALOTRY NEW FAD, EXPERTS SAY

WEST TOLEDO, OH (UPI)–Once common only among airline ter-
rorists and suburban housewives, religious zealotry has rapidly emerged as
the newest fad among pre-teen adolescents. It has quickly outpaced both
playing with the Nintendo and playing with the genitals as a primary
source of entertainment.

Just ask Sue Bitachi, 14, whose posters of Britney Spears have now been
replaced by the likenesses of the Ayatollah, Yassir Arrafat, and Pat
Robertson. "It's like totally cool," she says while cleaning a kamikaze
bomb and listening to Ricky Martin, "Oh migod! It's like so cool, because
all of you infidels will like totally suffer in the eternal, black pit of noth-
ingness when like the JIHAD totally paints the earth blood red with like
your intestines."

Experts believe that this fad is a result of the Golden Pacific Brewing
Company's Monthly Free Beer Party. The brewery, long known for it's
production of such fine products as oxygen and three of the four fundamental forces, has announced that it will donate several cases of it's bitter-
sweet Amber Ale and sublime Golden Lager to the pre-teen Holy War.

Jihad members rejoiced in the streets following the announcement.
One member rapturously lit himself on fire, knelt on the ground, and
chanted, "Oh holy lord! Sear my flesh! Destroy my soul! But, spare my
tongue to taste of the sweet Golden Pacific Brewing Company!"

STARVATION

LACK OF FOOD IMPLICATED IN STARVATION, STUDY SAYS

UPPER BOTSWANA, NJ (UPI)–Gathering today before an illustrious group of serial killers, pedophiles, and politicians, World Health Organization officials announced the results of a multi-million dollar, hour-long study of starvation in developing countries.

"Listen here, you fuckin' assholes," the report begins, "These people just don't have any fuckin' food! What the fuck is so hard to understand about that?!"

The report came as a surprise to Golden Pacific Brewing Company officials, whose past efforts at combating world hunger had drawn universal praise from such luminaries as former President Bill Clinton and ex-bowling superstar Bobby 'No Hands' McGoon.

"Frankly, we are shocked," stated GPBC president Bobby 'No Hands' McGoon, "We were positive that world hunger could be combated by offering free beer, pizza, and sausage to overweight, American freeloaders on the last Friday of every month. Apparently, we were mistaken."

Military officials were similarly caught off guard, and announced the immediate reduction of its nuclear arsenal. According to one spokesman, "Although we were led to believe by the GPBC in the curative potential of nuclear armageddon, in retrospect this was not the best means of alleviating world hunger. Damn you Golden Pacific Brewing Company! Damn you to hell!"

SLAVERY

JOBS DECLINE, SLAVERY ON THE RISE

NORTH TALLAHASSEE, AZ (UPI)–Films, such as "Roots", have notoriously popularized the glamorous life of slavery. What child hasn't fantasized of being chained and whipped then having their feet cut off for attempting to run away? Indeed, gruel served "Kunta Kintae-style" has all but replaced the "Sloppy Joe" on traditional school lunch menus.

Now, with an economy in decline, many are beginning to rediscover their childhood fantasy. Take for example, Martin Bergman, a former consultant with Dot-Com.com, now a male prostitute in the service of the Sultan of Brunei. "It's the best experience of my life!" stated Bergman during one of his hourly sodomy sessions, "They say if your ass doesn't hurt at the end of the day, you're not doing your job. I think the Sultan REALLY likes me! I'm living my dream, Man! I'm living my dream!!"

Helping people like Bergman transition into slavery is the Golden Pacific Brewing Company. The Brewery, long known for its ability to travel faster than light and communicate with the dead, has announced that it will continue to offer free beer, pizza and sausages to potential slaves on the last Friday of every month.

The White House has already glowingly endorsed the Brewery's endeavors. In a recent statement, President Bush proclaimed, "Although our past efforts at economic recovery have concentrated on defiling other nations and raping the environment, it now appears that guiding our citizens into slavery is the most obvious solution. God and the nation are indebted to you, Golden Pacific Brewing Company!"

BAKE OFF

ISLAMIC EXTREMISTS COMPETE IN BAKE-OFF

BANGOR, ME (UPI)–Islamic Extremists stormed the grounds of the "Little Debbie(tm) Snack Cake Bake-Off Competition" today and garnered first prize for their entry, the "Nutty Talibany Crunchy Pie". Just edged out of the running was Jerry Falwell and Pat Robertson's entry, "The Total Bigot Surprise".

The Christian Coalition's entry was clearly in the lead until their oven overheated, reducing their blanc mange to a smoldering pile of fattening carbohydrates. Photographs of the blackened blanc mange were reported to have shown the face of Satan floating in the smoke above. Commenting on the incident, Falwell is reported to have said, "I point the finger for this failure squarely at all of the self-righteous, intolerant, and bigoted bastards such as myself."

"This was an incident waiting to happen," according to Dr. Barry Sears, Zone-diet guru and Golden Pacific Brewing Company's head of latrines. "Little Debbie has been forcing people for years to eat a non-optimal ratio of proteins to carbohydrates. This has clearly spiked Insulin levels all across this great land of ours! An optimal ratio can clearly be found by consuming vast quantities of beer, sausages, and pizza at the Monthly Free Beer Party."

U.S. Leader's were reportedly elated at the announcement of another beer festival. According to one high-ranking official, "These extremists may rule the world of fattening carbohydrates, but the nation will persevere and obtain optimal health and nutrition. God Bless the Golden Pacific Brewing Company!"

THE MILLION DOLLAR GAME

I was running the Deep South Circuit the other day. I knocked off an easy competitor named Archibald Bearasol in the third round when a competitor from the D bracket came up and beat me in straight sets. Check and mate. I heard he went on to take the Deep South Regionals. He fights under many names. He is like Shang Tsung in the wind. He is not your father's Oldsmobile. Like a tree falling in the forest, like a particle in a box, like a virgin touched for the very first time, like a viiiirrrrrrgiiiiiiin, he took me to the moon and back. He told me, "Always treat your foosball table like your women. Get on it three times a day and take it to the hole." So, if you go to play Jack, make sure you bring a foosball and your VISA. Because, at Jack's they don't tolerate spinning the rods and they don't take American Express.

The Council of Immortal Warriors invites you to
participate in

MORTAL FOOSBALL
III

The Million Dollar Game

Now, the challenge continues....
Na Na Na Na
Hey
Hey
Hey
GOODBYE!!!

Wow! It's the Z! Sega.

This show was made possible by a grant from the Lulu Hull Lloyd Foundation.

And by members like you...

AFTERWORD

The end of the one, brings only the beginning of another.

CONCLUSIONS

Those who do not remember the past are condemned to repeat it.

About the Author

Charles Chulsoo Lee is a resident of Berkeley, CA where he spends his time pondering the essence of being, and occasionally does productive things as well. He hosts a weekly radio science program on KALX 90.7FM in Berkeley, CA and conducts research in neuroscience at the University of California at Berkeley.

Appendix I—Suggested Reading

Zen and the Art of Foosball: A Beginner's Guide to Table Soccer by Charles C.
Lee with David Richard and Attma Sharma

This book contains useful insights into life, zen, and most importantly
foosball. If you enjoyed reading *The Tao and The Engram*, then you will
enjoy reading my book on Zen.

REFERENCES

References to The Genetic Code: Historical Considerations

Asimov, Isaac. **The Genetic Code**, New York: Signet, 1962.

Borek, Ernest, **The Code of Life**, New York: Colubia University Press, 1965.

Grifiths, A.J., et.al , **Introduction to Genetic Analysis: 5th Ed.**, New York: W.H. Freeman and Co. 1993.

Woese, C., **The Genetic Code**, New York: Harper&Row, 1985

References to The Olfactory Code: Current Considerations.

Berghard A, Buck LB., Liman ER: **Evidence for distinct signaling mechanisms in two mammalian olfactory sense organs.** *Proc Natl Acad Sci USA* 1996, **93**: 2365-2369.

Breer H, Krieger J, Meinken C, Kiefer H, Strotman J: **Expression and functional analysis of olfactory receptors.** *Annals New York Acad Sci 1998,* **855**: 175-181.

Buck L, Axel R: **A novel multigene family may encode odorant receptors: A molecular basis for odorant recognition.** *Cell* 1991, **65**: 175-187.

Buck LB: **Information coding in the vertebrate olfactory system.** *Annu Rev Neuroscience* 1996, **19**: 517-544.

Clyne PJ, Warr CG, Freeman MR, Lessing D, Kim J: **A novel family of divergent seven-transmembrane proteins: Candidate odorant receptor in** *Drosophila. Neuron 1999,* **22**: 327-338.

Dodd J, Castellucci VF: **Smell and Taste: The Chemical Senses.** *Principles of Neural Science 3rd ed.,* 1991, 513-529.

Hadcock JR, Pausch MH: **Ligand screening of G-protein coupled receptors in Yeast.** *In: Haga T, Bernstein G, editors. G-Protein Coupled receptors.* 1999. New York, New York: CRC Press, p. 49-69.

Herrada G, Dulac C: **A Novel Family of Putative Pheromone Receptors in Mammals with a Topographically Organized and Sexually Dimorphic Distribution.** *Cell* 1997, **90**: 763-773.

Horowitz LF, Montmayeur JP, Echelard Y, Buck LB: **A genetic approach to trace Neural circuits.** *Proc. Natl, Acad. Sci. USA.* 1999, **96**:3194-99.

Krautwurst D, Yau KW, Reed RR: **Identification of ligands for olfactory Receptors by functional expression of a receptor library.** *Cell* 1998, **95**: 917-26.

Lurent G: **A systems perspective on early olfactory coding.** *Science* 1999, **286**: 723-28.

Malnick B, Hirono J, Sato T, Buck LB: **Combinatorial receptor codes for odors.** *Cell* 1999, **96**: 713-723.

Markham PN, LoGuidice J, Neyfakh AA: **Broad ligand specificity of the transcriptional regulator of the** *Bacillus subtilis* **multidrug transporter** *Biochem. Biophys. Res. Com.* 1997 **239**:269-72

Mitsuoka K, Hirai T, Murata K, Miyazawa A, Kidera A, Kimura Y, Fujiyoshi Y: **The structure of bacteriorhodopsin at 3.0 A resolution based on electron crystallography: implication of the charge distribution.** *J Mol Bio* 1999, **286**: 861-82.

Mombaerts P: **Molecular biology of odorant receptors in vertebrates.** *Annu Rev Neuroscience* 1999, **22**: 487-509.

Mori K, Nagao H, Yoshihara Y: **The olfactory bulb: Coding and processing of Odor molecule information.** *Science* 1999, **286**: 711-715.

Ngai J, Chess A, Dowling MM, Necles N, Macagno ER, Axel, R: **Coding of olfactory information: topography of odorant receptor expression in the catfish olfactory epithelium.** *Cell* 1993, **5**:667-80.

Reed RR: **Opening the window to odor space.** *Science* 1998, **279**: 193-194.

Ressler KJ, Sullivan SL, Buck LB: **A molecular dissection of spatial patterning in the olfactory system.** *Curr Opin Neurobiology* 1994, **4:** 588-96.

Sharon D, Glusman G, Pipel Y, Horn-Saban S, Lancet D: **Genome dynamics, evolution, and protein modeling in the olfactory receptor gene superfamily.** *Annals New York Acad Sci* 1998, **855:** 182-193.

Singer MS, Oliveira L, Vriend G, Shepherd GM: **Potential ligand-binding residues in rat olfactory receptors identified by correlated mutation analysis.** *Receptors and Channels* 1995, **3:** 89-95.

Singer MS, Shepherd GM: **Molecular modeling of ligand-receptor interactions in the OR5 olfactory receptor.** *NeuroReport* 1994, **5:** 1297-1300.

Unger VM, Schertler GFX: **Low resolution structure of bovine Rhodopsin determined by electron cryo-microscopy.** *Biophys J* 1995, **68:**1776-1786.

Zhang Y, Chou JH, Bradley J, Bargmann CI, Zinn K: **The** *Caenorhabditis elegans* **seven-transmembrane protein ODR-10 functions as an odorant receptor in mammalian cells.** *Proc Natl Acad Sci USA* 1997, **94:** 12162-12167.

Zhao H, Ivic L, Otaki J, Hashimoto M, Mikoshiba K, Firestein S: **Functional expression of a mammalian odorant receptor.** *Science* 1998, **279:** 237-242.

0-595-22465-2